Birds are Bodacious

Another adventure in the Alpha-Bitz™ Series

(Parents, you'll be happy to know this introduces over 50 new words for your children's growing minds!)

by

Joseph Fischer

Albatross are Acrobatic

Bluebirds are Bright

Cardinals are Charming

Ducklings are Dizzy

Eagles are Enchanting

Flamingos are Fluttering

Geese are Giddy

Hummingbirds are Humble

Ibis are Ideal

Jaegar's are Joyful

Kestrels are Kingly

Loons are Lively

Mallards are Mobile

Nutcrackers are Noble

Owls are Odd

Parrots are Perfect

Quail are Quirky

Ravens are Resilient

Storks are Steady

Toucan are Tactful

Ultramarine Grosbeaks are Uber

Vultures are Versatile

Woodpeckers are Wary

Xavier's Greenbul are veXed

Yellow Warblers
are Yellowish

Zero Birds Stayed Home for the Winter

What is your favorite bird?

(Draw it here)